POMPEII AND HERCULANEUM: THE LOST CITIES REBORN

In the shadow of Vesuvius

Alireza Minagar

Amazon

Copyright © 2024 Alireza Minagar

All rights reserved

The characters and events portrayed in this book are fictitious. Any similarity to real persons, living or dead, is coincidental and not intended by the author.

No part of this book may be reproduced, or stored in a retrieval system, or transmitted in any form or by any means, electronic, mechanical, photocopying, recording, or otherwise, without express written permission of the publisher.

ISBN-13: 9798327095793

Cover design by: Art Painter
Library of Congress Control Number: 2018675309
Printed in the United States of America

CONTENTS

Title Page

Copyright

Preface

Chapter 1: Exploring the Discovery of Pompeii and Herculaneum — 1

Chapter 2: Pompeii: The Lost City and Its Neighbor, Herculaneum — 6

Chapter 3: Pompeii and Herculaneum Archaeological Tours — 11

Chapter 4: Pompeii and Herculaneum History and Culture — 16

Chapter 5: Pompeii and Herculaneum Art and Architecture — 21

Chapter 6: Pompeii and Herculaneum Ancient Daily Life — 27

Chapter 7: Pompeii and Herculaneum Preservation and Restoration — 32

Chapter 8: Pompeii and Herculaneum Volcanic Detonation — 37

Chapter 9: Pompeii and Herculaneum Myths and Legends — 43

Chapter 10: Pompeii and Herculaneum Impact on Modern Society — 47

Chapter 11: Pompeii and Herculaneum Cuisine and Dining — 53

Chapter 12: Pompeii and Herculaneum Religious Practices and Beliefs — 57

Chapter 13: Conclusion — 64

PREFACE

The ancient cities of Pompeii and Herculaneum, forever frozen in time by the catastrophic eruption of Mount Vesuvius in 79 AD, continue to captivate our imaginations and enrich our understanding of the ancient world. These cities offer an unparalleled glimpse into the daily lives, culture, and society of ancient Rome, preserved under layers of volcanic ash and debris.

In this book, we embark on a journey through the history and locations of Pompeii and Herculaneum, exploring the architectural marvels, artistic achievements, and intricate details of everyday life that have been uncovered through meticulous archaeological efforts. From the grandiose temples and bustling marketplaces to the intimate settings of private homes, this book aims to provide a comprehensive view of these remarkable cities.

We delve into the religious practices, social dynamics, and economic activities that defined the lives of the residents of Pompeii and Herculaneum. Through vivid descriptions and insights drawn from the latest research, this book brings to life the stories of these ancient communities, whose legacy continues to inspire and educate us today.

As we explore the ruins and artifacts that have been meticulously preserved, we gain not only an appreciation for the resilience and ingenuity of the ancient Romans but also a deeper understanding of the human experience that transcends time. This book is dedicated to all who seek to learn about the rich history and cultural heritage of Pompeii and Herculaneum, inviting readers to discover the timeless lessons and enduring beauty of these ancient cities.

Disclaimer

The information presented in this book is based on extensive research and archaeological findings related to the ancient cities of Pompeii and Herculaneum. While every effort has been made to ensure the accuracy and completeness of the content, the author and publisher make no representations or warranties regarding the currentness, reliability, or suitability of the information contained herein.

This book is intended for educational and informational purposes only and should not be construed as professional advice. This is a fun book to read and by no means can be used as a scientific textbook or resource for any scientific or economic presentations or decisions. The author and publisher disclaim any liability for any loss or damage caused, directly or indirectly, by the use or reliance on the information presented in this book.

Readers are encouraged to conduct their own research and consult additional sources to gain a comprehensive understanding of the subject matter. The historical interpretation and insights offered in this book reflect the current state of knowledge and may evolve as new discoveries and scholarship emerge.

CHAPTER 1: EXPLORING THE DISCOVERY OF POMPEII AND HERCULANEUM

How were Pompeii and Herculaneum were Revealed? The uncovering of Pompeii and Herculaneum in the 18th century was a monumental moment in the field of archaeology, as it provided a preview into the daily lives and activities of the people who lived in these ancient Roman cities. The cities were sunken under sheets of ash and pumice after the outburst of Mount Vesuvius in 79 AD, sustaining them in an outstanding condition of preservation for over 1,900 years.

The initial excavations of Pompeii and Herculaneum were spearheaded by the Bourbon kings of Naples in the mid-18th century. Driven by a fervent desire to unearth the treasures hidden beneath the layers of volcanic ash, these monarchs embarked on a journey that would bring the ancient Roman world back to life. The excavations revealed a stunning array of artifacts, including exquisitely preserved frescoes, intricate mosaics, and the skeletal remains of buildings and streets that once bustled with activity. These findings opened a window into the artistic, architectural, and everyday life of the Romans, offering invaluable insights into their sophisticated society.

One of Pompeii's most celebrated discoveries is the Villa of the Mysteries. This villa stands as a testament to the artistic prowess of its time, adorned with breathtaking frescoes that depict enigmatic rituals and ceremonies, leaving historians and visitors alike in awe. In Herculaneum, the excavation of the Villa of the Papyri unearthed a priceless collection of ancient scrolls. These scrolls, preserving the literary and philosophical works of the Romans, have significantly enriched our understanding of their intellectual pursuits.

The endeavor to excavate and preserve Pompeii and Herculaneum has been an ongoing effort for over two centuries. Each layer of volcanic debris removed reveals new stories and insights into the lives of the ancient Romans. The cities, now iconic archaeological sites, draw tourists from across the globe. Visitors walk through the remarkably well-preserved ruins, gaining a tangible connection to the past and a deeper appreciation for the history and customs of ancient Rome.

The heritage of Pompeii and Herculaneum extends far beyond their historical and archaeological significance. These cities have profoundly inspired art, literature, and popular habits. They have inspired countless novels, films, and artworks, appealing to the imagination of populations worldwide. The tragic end of Pompeii and Herculaneum stands as a stark reminder of nature's might and the fleeting nature of human endeavors. Yet, in their ruin, these cities symbolize both the fragility and resilience of human civilization, enduring as poignant monuments to our shared heritage.

Importance of Pompeii and Herculaneum in Archaeology Pompeii and Herculaneum are two ancient Roman cities that were famously covered under volcanic ash and pumice stone when Mount Vesuvius erupted in 79 AD. These cities have since been excavated and have provided invaluable perceptions into the everyday life, values, and architecture of the Roman Empire. The importance of Pompeii and Herculaneum in archaeology cannot be overstated, as they offer a unique stare into the past and help us understand the ancient world in a way that would not be possible otherwise.

One of the key reasons why Pompeii and Herculaneum are so important in archaeology is their remarkable preservation. The volcanic ash that covered the cities acted as a natural time capsule, freezing them in time and protecting them from the elements. Accordingly, archaeologists have been able to discover incredibly well-preserved structures, artifacts, and even human remains, providing a detailed picture of life in ancient Rome.

In addition to their preservation, Pompeii and Herculaneum are also significant because they offer a rare squint into the daily lives of ancient Romans. From the layout of the cities to the artifacts found within them, we can learn about everything from the food they ate to the clothes they wore. This information helps us paint a more complete picture of Roman society and understand how people lived during this time period.

Furthermore, the art and architecture of Pompeii and Herculaneum are also crucial in understanding the ancient world. The cities were home to beautiful frescoes, mosaics, and sculptures that provide insights into Roman aesthetics and artistic techniques. By studying these works of art, we can gain a better understanding of Roman values and society, as well as the values and beliefs that were important to the people who lived there.

Overall, the prominence of Pompeii and Herculaneum in archaeology cannot be exaggerated. These cities provide a unique window into the past and offer treasured awareness into the casual life, rituals, and art of ancient Rome. By studying Pompeii and Herculaneum, we can learn more about the ancient world and gain a better understanding of how our modern society has been shaped by the past.

O verview of the Lost Cities
The lost cities of Pompeii and Herculaneum are two of the most well-known archaeological sites in the world, offering a quick look into the daily events of the ancient Romans. Stationed near the Bay of Naples in Italy, these cities were tragically interred under layers of volcanic dust and pumice whilst Mount Vesuvius erupted in 79 AD. Despite the devastation caused by the eruption, the preservation of these cities has provided valuable insights into Roman society, culture, and architecture.

Pompeii, the larger of the two cities, was an energetic profitable center with a populace of around 20,000 people. It was known for its thriving economy, vibrant street life, and impressive public buildings, such as the amphitheater and the Temple of Apollo. Herculaneum, in contrast, was a smaller more upscale residential town favored by the affluent elite. Its well-preserved buildings, intricate mosaics, and luxurious villas offer a flicker into the opulent lifestyle of the Roman aristocracy.

Visitors to Pompeii and Herculaneum can explore the ancient streets, houses, and public buildings that have been excavated over the centuries. Directed excursions are offered to assist people traverse the sprawling sites and learn more about the archeology and worldview of these lost cities. The ruins of Pompeii and Herculaneum also showcase the art and architecture of the Roman Empire, with beautifully preserved frescoes, sculptures, and mosaics that offer a window into the artistic tastes of the time.

In addition to their architectural and artistic wonders, Pompeii and Herculaneum bestow worthy perceptions into the daily beings and events of antique Romans. From what are left from ancient bakeries and taverns to the sustained bodies of citizens captured during the eruption, these cities offer a poignant reminder of the fragility of life and the power of nature. The preservation and restoration efforts at Pompeii and Herculaneum have ensured that these sites remain accessible to the public, allowing visitors to experience firsthand the impact of the volcanic eruption that forever changed the course of ages.

The legacy of Pompeii and Herculaneum extends far beyond their ancient ruins, influencing modern society in a variety of ways. From inspiring works of art and literature to shaping our understanding of ancient history, these lost cities continue to captivate the imagination of people around the world. The cuisine, religious practices, and beliefs of the ancient Romans are also on display at Pompeii and Herculaneum, offering a fascinating glimpse into the daily rituals and traditions of this ancient civilization. If you have a passion for history, a keen interest in art, or a simple curiosity about ancient civilizations, visiting Pompeii and Herculaneum will offer you an unforgettable and enriching journey through time. These ancient cities, frozen in the past and time by the disastrous volcanic explosion of Mount Vesuvius, provide a distinctive window into the daily lives, culture, and artistry of their inhabitants. The well-preserved ruins and intricate frescoes tell stories that resonate across millennia, making your exploration both captivating and profoundly educational. A trip to these archaeological wonders is not just a visit; it is an immersive experience that brings retrospect to life.

CHAPTER 2: POMPEII: THE LOST CITY AND ITS NEIGHBOR, HERCULANEUM

Location and Geography of Pompeii and Herculaneum

Located in the region of Campania in southern Italy, Pompeii and Herculaneum are two ancient Roman cities that were hidden under deposits of volcanic ash and pumice when Mount Vesuvius ejected in 79 AD. The cities are situated near the Bay of Naples, with Pompeii lying about 5 miles southeast of the volcano and Herculaneum about 10 miles to the west. The proximity to Mount Vesuvius played a crucial role in the preservation of these cities, as the volcanic ash acted as a time capsule, freezing the cities in time for nearly two millennia.

The geography of Pompeii and Herculaneum is characterized by their coastal location, with stunning visions of the Bay of Naples and the immediate mountains. The cities were thriving centers of trade and commerce, with easy access to the sea for shipping goods and materials. The fertile volcanic soil in the region also allowed for abundant agriculture, with vineyards and olive groves dotting the landscape. The mild Mediterranean climate of the area made it an ideal location for ancient Roman settlements.

The layout of Pompeii and Herculaneum reflects their Roman origins, with a grid-based street plan and well-preserved public buildings such as temples, theaters, and baths. The architecture of the cities is a mix of Roman and Greek styles, with grand villas featuring intricate mosaics and frescoes, and public buildings adorned with marble statues and columns. The streets of Pompeii and Herculaneum were lined with shops and taverns, bustling with activity and commerce.

The regular life of the citizens of Pompeii and Herculaneum revolved around their social, religious, and economic activities. The cities were home to a diverse population of Romans, Greeks, and other cultures, with a mix of artisans, merchants, and wealthy landowners. The residents of Pompeii and Herculaneum enjoyed a rich cultural life, with theaters, public baths, and temples serving as gathering places for social and religious events.

Despite the tragic fate that befell Pompeii and Herculaneum with the exhalation of Mount Vesuvius, the cities have left a lasting impact on modern society. The archaeological excavations of Pompeii and Herculaneum have provided worthwhile awareness into dated Roman life, art, and architecture. The preservation and restoration efforts at the sites continue to uncover new discoveries and shed light on the daily lives of the people who once inhabited these lost cities.

Relationship Between Pompeii and Herculaneum
The relationship between Pompeii and Herculaneum is one of interconnectedness and shared background that dates to ancient times. These two neighboring cities, located near the Bay of Naples in Italy, were both tragically demolished by the outburst of Mount Vesuvius in 79 AD. Despite their proximity, the

two cities had discrete properties and differentiations that made them dissimilar and unique in their own place.

Pompeii, the larger and more well-known of the two cities, was a bustling commercial hub with a population of around 11,000 people. It was known for its extravagant frescoes, grand villas, and bustling markets. Herculaneum, conversely, was a smaller, wealthier city with a inhabitant of nearly 4,000 individuals. It was known for its luxurious waterfront villas and its proximity to the sea.

Despite their differences, Pompeii and Herculaneum shared many similarities in terms of their architecture, art, and daily life. Both cities were heavily persuaded by Greek and Roman culture, and their ruins offer a glimpse into the daily lives of ancient Romans. The unearthing of these cities has provided invaluable insights into ancient Roman society, from their religious practices and beliefs to their cuisine and dining habits.

The volcanic outburst that interred Pompeii and Herculaneum preserved these cities in a state of suspended animation, allowing archaeologists to uncover a wealth of information about their social values and fabric. The ongoing preservation and restoration efforts at both sites have ensured that future generations will be able to learn from and appreciate these ancient cities.

Today, Pompeii and Herculaneum continue to captivate visitors from around the world with their art, architecture, and fascinating history. The impact of these lost cities on modern society is profound, as they serve as a prompt of the vulnerability of social civilization in the face of natural disasters. The myths and legends surrounding the destruction of Pompeii and Herculaneum only add to their allure, making them a must-see destination for anyone interested in ancient history and archaeology.

Differences in Architecture and Layout
Pompeii and Herculaneum, two early Roman cities interred by the explosion and outburst of Mount Vesuvius in 79 AD, offer a fascinating glance into the past. While both cities share similarities in terms of their chronicle and customs, there are distinct differences in their architecture and layout that reflect the unique characteristics of each city.

One of the most striking contrasts between Pompeii and Herculaneum is their architectural designs. Pompeii is known for its grand public buildings, such as the Forum and the amphitheater, which showcase the wealth and power of the city. In contrast, Herculaneum is characterized by its luxurious villas, many of which feature intricate mosaics and frescoes that depict scenes from daily life. The layout of Herculaneum is also more compact and orderly compared to the labyrinthine streets of Pompeii.

Another key difference between the two cities lies in their conservation and rebuilding attempts. Pompeii has undergone extensive restoration work since its reawakening in the 18th century, which has helped to preserve many of its iconic structures. In contrast, Herculaneum has been less heavily restored, giving visitors a more authentic sense of what the city would have looked like before its destruction.

The volcanic eruption's impact on daily life in Pompeii and Herculaneum is strikingly evident in their architecture and urban layout. In Pompeii, the city was submerged under a packed layer of ash and pumice, which remarkably preserved its structures and artifacts. Conversely, Herculaneum was engulfed by a pyroclastic flow, causing its structures to collapse and be preserved in a different manner. This contrast in preservation has provided unique insights into the daily lives of the residents of each city.

Despite these preservation differences, both Pompeii and Herculaneum offer invaluable eyefuls into the ancient Roman world. Exploring their architecture and urban design allows visitors to gain a profound understanding of the lives of those who lived over two millennia ago. Whether your interests lie in art and architecture, the intricacies of daily life, or the dramatic impact of natural disasters, both cities have something captivating to offer. The ruins of Pompeii and Herculaneum stand as enduring testimonies to a bygone era, inviting exploration and reflection on the past.

CHAPTER 3: POMPEII AND HERCULANEUM ARCHAEOLOGICAL TOURS

Popular Sites to Visit in Pompeii and Herculaneum
Pompeii and Herculaneum are two ancient Roman cities that were famously hidden by the outbreak of Mount Vesuvius in 79 AD. Today, these archaeological sites offer an intriguing peek into the each day lives of the people who lived there over two thousand years ago. Both cities are admired aims and locations for visitors and history admirers alike, with numerous sites to visit and explore.

One of the most popular sites to visit in Pompeii is the Forum, the center ground of political, religious, and social life in the city. Here, visitors can see the remains of temples, basilicas, and government buildings, as well as the marketplace where merchants would have sold their goods. The Forum provides a window into the public life of Pompeii and the importance of civic spaces in Roman society.

In Herculaneum, one of the must-see sites is the Villa of the Papyri, a luxurious seaside villa that was hidden under a thick tier of volcanic ash. This villa is famous for its collection of ancient scrolls, which were preserved by the volcanic discharge event and provide appreciated awareness of the Roman literature and philosophy. The Villa of the Papyri is a testament to the wealth and sophistication of Herculaneum's elite residents.

Another popular site in Pompeii is the House of the Vettii, a superbly conserved mansion that offers a view into the private existences of the city's wealthy citizens. This house is renowned for its sophisticated frescoes, which portray displays from mythology, scenery, and daily life. The House of the Vettii showcases the artistic and architectural prowess of Pompeii's craftsmen and the opulent lifestyle of its upper class.

In both Pompeii and Herculaneum, visitors can also explore the ancient bathhouses, theaters, and amphitheaters that were central to Roman social and cultural life. These sites provide insight into the leisure activities and entertainment enjoyed by the cities' residents, as well as the architectural innovations of the Roman Empire. By visiting these popular sites, tourists can gain a deeper understanding of the antiquity, culture, and daily life of Pompeii and Herculaneum before they were tragically destroyed by the spew of Mount Vesuvius.

G uided Tours and Self-Guided Tours Options
When visiting the classical municipalities of Pompeii and Herculaneum, there are a variety of tour options available to suit different preferences and interests. Guided tours are a widespread choice for those who are interested in having a comprehensive and informative experience led by experienced experts. These tours typically include a guide who will lead visitors through the key archaeological sites, providing historical context and insights into the daily life of the ancient inhabitants.

For visitors and tourists who express desire for private or autonomous sightseeing and search experience, self-guided expeditions are also a viable option. Visitors can explore the ruins at their own pace, using guidebooks or audio guides to learn about the history and significance of the various structures and artifacts. Self-guided tours allow for more flexibility and freedom, enabling visitors to concentrate on identifiable areas of curiosity or spend more time at sites.

Guided tours offer the advantage of having a knowledgeable guide who can provide detailed explanations and answer questions along the way. These tours often follow a set itinerary, ensuring that visitors see all the major highlights of Pompeii and Herculaneum. Guides may also share interesting anecdotes and stories about the cities, bringing the ancient ruins to life and making the experience more engaging and memorable.

Self-guided tours, on the other hand, allow visitors to explore the sites at their own rate and emphasis on areas that interest them the most. While these tours may not offer the same level of detailed information as guided tours, they provide a more personalized and flexible experience. Visitors can take their time to appreciate the architecture, artwork, and everyday artifacts of Pompeii and Herculaneum without feeling rushed or constrained by a group tour schedule.

Ultimately, whether you choose a guided tour or a self-guided tour, visiting Pompeii and Herculaneum is a unique and unforgettable experience that offers a fascinating sight into the daily life, art, architecture, and collective identity of ancient Roman society. By exploring these well-preserved ruins, visitors can gain a deeper understanding of the past and significance of these lost cities and appreciate the impact they have had on modern society. Whether you are a chronicle admirer, an art supporter, or simply curious about the annals, Pompeii and Herculaneum have something to present to everyone.

Tips for Visiting the Archaeological Sites
When visiting the archaeological sites of Pompeii and Herculaneum, a few practical tips can help you make the most of your experience. Firstly, wearing comfortable shoes and clothing is essential, as these sites are extensive and require a lot of walking and exploration. Given the size of the sites and the potential for hot weather during the summer months, it's also important to bring sunscreen, a hat, and plenty of water to stay hydrated. Proper preparation will ensure that your visit is not only enjoyable but also comfortable, allowing you to fully immerse yourself in the rich memoir and remarkable preservation of these ancient cities.

Another notable pointer is to arrive early in the day to prevent the crowds and the heat. The sites can get very busy, especially during peak tourist season, so getting an early start will allow you to enjoy the sites at a more leisurely pace. Additionally, hiring a guide or joining a guided tour can provide valuable insights and information about the provenance and significance of the sites.

As you explore the ruins of Pompeii and Herculaneum, take the time to appreciate the intricate art and architecture that has been preserved for centuries. From superbly conserved frescoes to elaborate mosaics, these locations present the lineage of ancient Rome and its citizens. Be sure to take plenty of photos, but also take moments to simply soak in the antiquities and atmosphere of these astonishing municipalities.

It's also crucial to respect the sites and adhere to any rules or regulations in place to protect them. Avoid touching or removing any artifacts or ruins and be wary of your surroundings to avoid causing damage. By treating these locations with care and respect, you contribute to the preservation of these historical treasures for future generations to learn from and appreciate.

Lastly, take the time to learn together about the myths, legends, and stories that surround these ancient cities. From the tragic tale of Mount Vesuvius's outflow to the everyday lives of the inhabitants, there is a wealth of background to explore and understand. Approach your visit with curiosity and an open mind to gain a deeper appreciation for the rich cultural heritage of Pompeii and Herculaneum. This thoughtful engagement will enrich your experience, allowing you to connect more profoundly with the past and the remarkable stories these ancient cities must tell.

CHAPTER 4: POMPEII AND HERCULANEUM HISTORY AND CULTURE

Earliest Annals of Pompeii and Herculaneum
The ancient saga of Pompeii and Herculaneum is a fascinating tale of two thriving Roman cities that were tragically enshrouded by the volcanic ash of Mount Vesuvius in 79 AD. Once busy and bubbling with life and events, now they only serve as surviving reminders of the nature versus mankind.

Pompeii, known as the "lost city," was a prosperous commercial center situated near the Bay of Naples. It was an admired destination for prosperous Romans pursuing leisureliness and relaxation. The city boasted elaborate villas, community baths, theaters, and temples devoted to diverse gods and goddesses. Pompeii's well-preserved ruins provide worthy perceptions into ancient Roman architecture and urban development.

Herculaneum, positioned just a few kilometers from Pompeii, was a smaller but equally important city. It was known for its wealthy residents and luxurious waterfront villas. The city's ruins reveal intricate mosaics, frescoes, and artifacts that offer a detailed explanation as how people of those days and years lived and survived. Herculaneum was also home to a significant library, which contained scrolls and manuscripts that provide valuable information about ancient Roman social values and society fabrics.

The volcanic event of Mount Vesuvius in 79 AD buried both Pompeii and Herculaneum under deposits of ash and pumice, keeping them outstandingly for centuries. Their revelations in the 18th century ignited a renewed fascination with ancient Roman genealogy and heritage. Today, Pompeii and Herculaneum are popular tourist destinations, drawing visitors from around the globe eager to explore their well-preserved ruins and learn about their ancient past.

The archaeological sites of Pompeii and Herculaneum offer a unique window into the daily lives of ancient Romans. Visitors can wander through the remains of ancient homes, shops, and public buildings, gaining valuable insights into the social, economic, and cultural dynamics of these cities. The art and architecture of Pompeii and Herculaneum reflect the tastes and preferences of their inhabitants, showcasing a captivating blend of Roman, Greek, and Etruscan impressions. From the vibrant frescoes adorning the walls of villas to the intricate mosaics decorating public spaces, these cities are a treasure trove of ancient art and craftsmanship.

Beyond their architectural wonders, Pompeii and Herculaneum provide a view to the ordinary life of its people prior to the volcanic explosion. Temples dedicated to various gods and goddesses, along with shrines and altars scattered throughout the cities, reveal the spiritual life of their inhabitants. The volcanic upheaval that embedded these cities also left behind a wealth of myths and legends, which have captivated historians and archaeologists for centuries.

Exploring Pompeii and Herculaneum is not just about observing ancient ruins; it's about connecting with the past and understanding the lives of people who lived over two thousand years ago. The preservation of these sites allows us to walk through the past, offering a tangible link to a world long gone yet vividly brought to life through their remnants.

I ntellectual Impacts in Pompeii and Herculaneum
Cultural stimuli played a significant role in shaping the societies of Pompeii and Herculaneum, two vibrant archaic Roman cities submerged by the tragic venting of Mount Vesuvius in 79 AD. These cities were thriving centers of commerce, art, and traditions, with residents influenced by a rich tapestry of traditions from across the Roman Empire.

One of the most noticeable cultural issues in Pompeii and Herculaneum was Roman religion. The inhabitants worshipped a pantheon of gods and goddesses, with temples dedicated to deities such as Jupiter, Venus, and Mercury. Religious practices and beliefs were central to daily life, with rituals and ceremonies practiced honoring the gods and seek their support.

The art and architecture of Pompeii and Herculaneum were also profoundly signified by Roman communal practices. These cities boasted grand public buildings, including theaters, amphitheaters, and bathhouses, alongside luxurious villas adorned with intricate frescoes and mosaics. Roman artists and architects drew inspiration from classical Greek and Etruscan styles, creating a unique blend of commands that remain evident in the archaeological remains today.

Daily life in Pompeii and Herculaneum was a mosaic of cultural reaches, noticed in everything from the food people ate to the clothes they displayed. These cities were melting pots of different social habits, with residents from across the Roman Empire living and working side by side. This assortment is mirrored in the archaeological evidence, which reveals imported goods and exotic foods enjoyed by the inhabitants.

The cultural heritage of Pompeii and Herculaneum continues to resonate in modern society. These ancient cities have inspired countless artists, writers, and filmmakers, who have drawn on their rich history and ancestry in their works. Pompeii and Herculaneum remain prevalent tourist destinations, attracting visitors from all over the globe who come to explore the ruins and learn about their fascinating past.

The preeminence of Pompeii and Herculaneum extends beyond their historical significance; they offer a window into the complex and interconnected world of ancient Rome. The preservation of these cities allows us to understand better the cultural, social, and economic dynamics that shaped the lives of their residents, providing a profound connection to our shared human heritage.

L egacy of Pompeii and Herculaneum in History
The legacy of Pompeii and Herculaneum is one that persists to attract and intrigue scholars, historians, and the everyone alike. Through ongoing archaeological excavations, we can piece together the puzzle of what life was like in these bustling cities nearly two thousand years ago.

Pompeii and Herculaneum offer a unique peek into the past, allowing us to walk the streets and enter the homes of ancient Romans. The well-preserved ruins of these cities provide a snapshot of daily life, revealing details about everything from food and clothing to religious practices and social customs. Pompeii has become an icon of the strength and valor of the Roman Empire, showcasing the wealth and sophistication of its inhabitants.

The art and architecture of Pompeii and Herculaneum are also of great importance in understanding the cultural achievements of the Roman world. From intricate frescoes and mosaics to grand villas and public buildings, these cities were a hub of artistic activity. The motivation of Greek and Roman styles can be seen throughout the ruins, demonstrating the rich tapestry of dominances that modeled the visual arts of the time.

In addition to their cultural significance, the preservation and restoration efforts at Pompeii and Herculaneum have played a crucial role in ensuring that these ancient cities are not lost to history. Through careful excavation and conservation work, archaeologists have been able to uncover and protect countless treasures, allowing future generations to continue learning from and appreciating these remarkable sites.

The impact of Pompeii and Herculaneum on modern society cannot be overstated. Their story has inspired countless works of art, literature, and film, while also serving as a cautionary tale about the power of nature and the fragility of human civilization. By exploring the anecdote, art, and traditional practices of these lost cities, we can connect with our ancient past and gain a deeper appreciation for the enduring legacy of Pompeii and Herculaneum.

CHAPTER 5: POMPEII AND HERCULANEUM ART AND ARCHITECTURE

Architectural Styles in Pompeii and Herculaneum
The cities of Pompeii and Herculaneum are recognized for their well-preserved ancient architecture, providing us with significant clues to the events and lifestyle prior to the devastating emission of Mount Vesuvius in 79 AD. The architectural styles found in these cities give us a decent sense about these people's preferences and view of life.

One of the most prominent architectural styles in Pompeii and Herculaneum is the Roman style, characterized by its use of brick, concrete, and marble. Roman architecture was known for its grandeur and sophistication, with intricate details and decorative elements adorning buildings, temples, and public spaces. The Roman hue and presence can be witnessed in the layout of the cities, with wide streets, public baths, and amphitheaters designed to accommodate large crowds.

Another architectural panache found in Pompeii and Herculaneum is the Greek fashion, which was prevalent in the region due to its proximity to Greece. Greek architecture was exemplified by its exploit of columns, pediments, and friezes, constructing a sense of harmony and balance in buildings. The impetus of Greek architecture can be observed in the design of temples, homes, and public erections in both cities.

In addition to Roman and Greek impressions, Pompeii and Herculaneum also exhibit components of Etruscan architecture, reflecting the cultural exchange and trade that occurred in the region. Etruscan architecture was known for its use of terracotta and decorative elements, such as painted frescoes and sculptures. The Etruscan inducement can be perceived in the ornate facades of buildings, as well as the design of tombs and monuments.

The architectural styles in Pompeii and Herculaneum offer a unique perspective on the ancient world, showcasing the artistic and cultural achievements of the time. By studying the buildings, temples, and public spaces of these cities, archaeologists and historians can gain a better understanding of the daily lives, beliefs, and practices of the people who lived there. The preservation and restoration efforts in Pompeii and Herculaneum have ensured that these architectural treasures will continue to inspire and educate future generations about the rich timeline and social ethos of the ancient world.

F amous Artifacts and Artworks Found in the Cities
In the cities of Pompeii and Herculaneum, numerous famous artifacts and artworks have been unearthed, offering a profound glimmer into the rich timeline and legacy of these ancient Roman cities. These discoveries provide instrumental awareness of the daily life, art, architecture, and religious practices of the inhabitants before the catastrophic flux of Mount Vesuvius in 79 AD.

One of the most recognized artifacts found in Pompeii is the Villa of the Mysteries. This exceptionally well-preserved Roman villa is renowned for its stunning frescoes, which depict intricate scenes of ancient Roman religious rituals. These frescoes offer a rare and vivid portrayal of the religious beliefs and practices of the ancient Romans, underscoring the significant role spirituality played in their daily lives.

Another notable finding is the House of the Faun, one of the greatest and most extraordinary homes in Pompeii. The house is famous for its elaborate mosaics, including the Alexander Mosaic, which depicts a dramatic act from the Battle of Issus between Alexander the Great and King Darius III. This artwork exemplifies the skill and artistry of Roman craftsmen and presents insights into the cultural and historical dominations that shaped Pompeian society.

In Herculaneum, the Villa of the Papyri is a remarkable archaeological find. This villa housed an extensive library of papyrus scrolls, many of which have been partially preserved. The scrolls, containing works of Greek and Latin literature, offer a unique window into the intellectual pursuits and literary legacy of the ancient Romans.

Artifacts such as these not only highlight the artistic and architectural achievements of Pompeii and Herculaneum but also reflect the everyday activities and interests of their residents. The unveiling of household items, tools, and personal belongings provides a tangible connection to the lives of ordinary people, revealing details about their domestic routines, culinary practices, and social interactions.

Religious artifacts, including statues, altars, and temple remnants, further illustrate the spiritual life of these ancient cities. Temples dedicated to gods such as Jupiter, Venus, and Mercury, along with various household shrines, demonstrate the pervasiveness of religious devotion and the diversity of worship practices in Roman society.

The preservation of Pompeii and Herculaneum allows modern visitors and scholars to explore the complexity and richness of ancient Roman life. These cities stand as enduring testaments to the cultural, artistic, and intellectual achievements of their time, offering a treasure trove of knowledge and inspiration for generations to come.

In Herculaneum, one of the most famous artworks is the Herculaneum Women, a collection of beautifully preserved marble sculptures depicting the elegant and graceful women of Herculaneum. These sculptures offer a look into the fashion and beauty standards of the ancient Roman women, showcasing their intricate hairstyles, jewelry, and clothing.

Another famous artifact found in Pompeii is the House of the Faun, a grand Roman villa known for its impressive mosaic floors, including the renowned Alexander Mosaic illustrating the Battle of Issus. The House of the Faun presents constructive visions into the art and architecture of ancient Pompeii, showcasing the wealth and sophistication of its inhabitants.

In Herculaneum, the House of the Wooden Partition is another famous archaeological site known for its intricate wooden partition that once separated the rooms of the villa. This artifact showcases the craftsmanship and attention to detail of the ancient Roman artisans, highlighting the luxurious living standards of the elite residents of Herculaneum.

Overall, the famous artifacts and artworks found in Pompeii and Herculaneum offer a valuable look into the daily life, art, architecture, and religious practices of the ancient Roman cities before they were tragically buried by the activity of Mount Vesuvius. These artifacts provide an exceptional prospect to learn about the rich past and origins of Pompeii and Herculaneum, casting light on the supremacy of the volcanic emission on these once-thriving cities.

I mpact of Greek and Roman Art in Pompeii and Herculaneum In the timeworn cities of Pompeii and Herculaneum, the drive of Greek and Roman art can be seen throughout the architectural structures, sculptures, and frescoes that have been unearthed over the centuries. These two cities were once thriving hubs of trade and commerce, drawing persuasions from numerous backgrounds and civilizations. The art found in Pompeii and Herculaneum reflects the fusion of Greek and Roman styles, showcasing the mastery of craftsmanship and artistic expression.

One of the key motivations of Greek and Roman art in Pompeii and Herculaneum is the architectural design of public buildings and private residences. The use of columns, arches, and intricate detailing in the construction of temples, theaters, and villas is reminiscent of Roman architecture, while the incorporation of marble statues and decorative elements reflects the Greek dominance on art and design. The blending of these styles created a unique aesthetic that defined the visual landscape of these ancient cities.

In addition to architecture, the sculptures found in Pompeii and Herculaneum also spotlight the motivation of Greek and Roman art. The lifelike depictions of human figures, mythological scenes, and deities reflect the mastery of sculptors in capturing the beauty and emotion of their subjects. The use of marble and bronze to create these sculptures further highlights the skill and craftsmanship of ancient artists in these cities.

The frescoes that adorn the walls of buildings in Pompeii and Herculaneum also demonstrate the prestige of Greek and Roman art in their intricate designs and vibrant colors. These wall paintings often depict scenes from daily life, mythology, and religious beliefs, showcasing the artistic talent and storytelling abilities of the ancient inhabitants. The blending of Greek and Roman artistic techniques in these frescoes created a unique visual language that continues to captivate visitors to this day.

Overall, the reach of Greek and Roman art in Pompeii and Herculaneum is evident in the architecture, sculptures, and frescoes that have been uncovered through archaeological excavations. The fusion of these artistic styles created a visual landscape that reflected the cultural richness and diversity of these ancient cities, leaving behind a legacy of artistic excellence that continues to inspire and awe visitors from around the world.

CHAPTER 6: POMPEII AND HERCULANEUM ANCIENT DAILY LIFE

Social Formation and Classes in Pompeii and Herculaneum The cities of Pompeii and Herculaneum were vibrant hubs of ancient Roman society, each with its own unique social structure and classes. In both cities, social status was largely determined by one's wealth, occupation, and family background. The elite class in Pompeii and Herculaneum consisted of wealthy landowners, businessmen, and government officials who held significant power and governance in society. These individuals lived in grand villas adorned with lavish decorations and enjoyed a life of luxury and privilege.

Below the elite class were the middle-class citizens, who constituted the bulk of the inhabitants in Pompeii and Herculaneum. This social stratum included merchants, craftsmen, and professionals who worked in various industries such as pottery, agriculture, and construction. While not as wealthy or powerful as the elite, the middle class enjoyed a comfortable lifestyle and had access to education and leisure activities.

At the underneath of the social pyramid were the lower-class residents of Pompeii and Herculaneum, who were primarily slaves, freedmen, and laborers. These individuals performed the manual labor necessary for the functioning of the cities, such as cleaning, farming, and construction. Despite their low social status, some slaves were able to earn their freedom and become freedmen, allowing them to live independently and pursue their own livelihoods.

The social structure of Pompeii and Herculaneum was also commanded by factors such as gender and ethnicity. Women in both cities held a subordinate position to men and were required to fulfill established positions as wives, mothers, and homemakers. Slaves and freedmen of non-Roman descent faced discrimination and limited opportunities for advancement in society.

Overall, the social structure and classes in Pompeii and Herculaneum were complex and hierarchical, reflecting the diverse and interconnected nature of ancient Roman society. By studying the social dynamics of these cities, we can gain valuable insights into the daily lives, relationships, and power dynamics of the people who called Pompeii and Herculaneum home.

D aily Activities and Routines of the Citizens
In the ancient cities of Pompeii and Herculaneum, the daily activities and routines of the citizens were quite similar to those of modern-day society, albeit with some unique differences. The citizens of both cities followed a routine that revolved around work, family, and social activities.

One of the most frequent daily events for the citizens of Pompeii and Herculaneum was work. Many of the citizens were involved in agriculture, trade, or craftsmanship. Farmers would wake up early to tend to their fields, while traders would open their shops in the bustling marketplaces. Craftsmen would spend their days creating pottery, jewelry, and other goods to sell to the citizens of the cities.

Family life was also an essential share of daily routines in Pompeii and Herculaneum. Families would assemble for meals, share stories, and pass time together in their homes. Children would attend school or help their parents with chores, while parents would work to provide for their families. The strong sense of community in both cities meant that families often relied on each other for support and companionship.

Social activities were another fundamental attribute of regular life in Pompeii and Herculaneum. Citizens would gather in the public baths, theaters, and temples to socialize, relax, and worship. The citizens of both cities enjoyed attending plays, gladiator games, and religious ceremonies to unwind and connect with their fellow citizens.

Despite the similarities in daily routines, there were also differences between the citizens of Pompeii and Herculaneum. For example, the citizens of Pompeii were known for their love of lavish feasts and extravagant parties, while the citizens of Herculaneum were more focused on intellectual pursuits and philosophical discussions. These differences added to the unique character of each city and enriched the daily lives of their citizens. By exploring the work, family life, and social activities of these citizens, we can gain a deeper understanding of the culture and society of these lost cities.

F ood, Clothing, and Entertainment in the Cities
Food, clothing, and entertainment were essential aspects of daily life in the bygone enclaves of Pompeii and Herculaneum. These bustling urban centers were filled with

a diverse array of culinary delights, fashionable attire, and lively entertainment options that catered to the tastes of their cosmopolitan populations.

In terms of food, both Pompeii and Herculaneum were known for their vibrant marketplaces and bustling street food scene. Locals could indulge in a variety of culinary offerings, from freshly baked bread and aromatic spices to succulent meats and flavorful wines. Seafood was particularly popular in these coastal cities, with fish and shellfish being staples of the local diet. Archaeological excavations have uncovered numerous food-related artifacts, such as cooking utensils, food storage containers, and even carbonized remains of ancient meals, providing valuable insights into the gastronomic preferences of the residents.

Clothing was another important aspect of daily life in Pompeii and Herculaneum. The cities were renowned for their thriving textile industry, producing a wide range of garments made from luxurious fabrics such as silk, wool, and linen. Fashion played a significant role in social status and identity, with individuals dressing to impress and showcase their wealth and taste. Artifacts such as jewelry, shoes, and clothing accessories have been unearthed in archaeological digs, providing valuable clues about the sartorial choices of the ancient inhabitants.

Entertainment options were plentiful in Pompeii and Herculaneum, with theaters, amphitheaters, and public baths serving as popular gathering spots for socializing and recreation. The cities were home to a vibrant cultural scene, with performances of plays, musical concerts, and gladiatorial contests drawing large crowds. In addition, residents could relax and unwind in the numerous public gardens, taverns, and brothels that dotted the urban landscape. These leisure activities provided a welcome respite from the rigors of daily life and offered residents a chance to socialize and connect with one another.

In particular, the cities of Pompeii and Herculaneum were vibrant hubs of food, clothing, and entertainment, offering residents a rich tapestry of cultural experiences. From the provocative fragrances of street food booths to the elegant fashions on display in the bustling marketplaces, these ancient cities were a feast for the senses. By exploring the archaeological remains and artifacts left behind, we can gain a deeper understanding of the daily lives and customs of the people who once called Pompeii and Herculaneum home.

CHAPTER 7: POMPEII AND HERCULANEUM PRESERVATION AND RESTORATION

Efforts to Preserve and Restore the Archaeological Sites Preserving and restoring the archaeological locations of Pompeii and Herculaneum is crucial in order to guarantee that future peers can continue to understand from and realize these ancient cities. The preservation efforts are aimed at protecting the ruins from further deterioration caused by natural elements, such as weather and erosion, as well as human activities, such as vandalism and over-tourism.

One of the main challenges in preserving and restoring the archaeological sites is striking a balance between allowing visitors to experience the long-lost but unforgotten ancient cities firsthand and protecting the fragile ruins from damage. To address this challenge, conservationists have implemented measures such as limiting the number of visitors allowed in certain areas, installing protective barriers around important structures, and using advanced technologies, such as drones and 3D scanning, to monitor the condition of the ruins.

In addition to physical preservation efforts, there are also ongoing conservation projects aimed at restoring and reconstructing parts of the cities that have been damaged or destroyed over time. These projects involve meticulous research, excavation, and reconstruction work, with the goal of recreating the cities as accurately as possible based on historical evidence and archaeological findings.

The preservation and restoration efforts at Pompeii and Herculaneum are not only important for protecting the physical remains of the time-honored cities, but also for preserving the cultural heritage and historical significance of these sites. By ensuring that the ruins are properly maintained and accessible to the public, we can continue to learn about the daily life, art, architecture, and religious practices of the ancient inhabitants of Pompeii and Herculaneum.

In conclusion, the efforts to preserve and restore the archaeological sites of Pompeii and Herculaneum are essential for safeguarding these invaluable treasures for future generations. Through careful conservation and restoration work, we can ensure that the legacy of these lost cities will continue to inspire and educate people from all over the world for years to come.

C hallenges in Maintaining the Ruins
Maintaining the ruins of Pompeii and Herculaneum presents a unique set of challenges due to the delicate nature of these ancient archaeological sites. The first challenge comes from the sheer size and complexity of the ruins themselves. Pompeii and Herculaneum are vast sites, with numerous buildings, streets, and artifacts that need to be carefully preserved and protected. This requires a dedicated team of archaeologists, conservators, and other experts to constantly monitor and maintain the ruins.

Another challenge in maintaining the ruins of Pompeii and Herculaneum is the threat of natural disasters. Both cities were submerged under deposits of volcanic ash and pumice during the devastating outburst of Mount Vesuvius in 79 AD. Today, they are still at risk of further damage from earthquakes, landslides, and other geological events. Efforts to protect the ruins from these potential disasters include structural reinforcements, monitoring systems, and emergency response plans.

One of the greatest encounters in retaining the ruins of Pompeii and Herculaneum is the pressure of tourism. Millions of visitors flock to these archaic sites each year, eager to search the well-preserved remains and learn about the background of the cities. While tourism is essential for funding conservation efforts, it also brings with it the risk of damage from foot traffic, vandalism, and theft. To mitigate these risks, strict rules and regulations are in place to protect the ruins and ensure that they can be enjoyed by future generations.

Preserving the delicate frescoes, mosaics, and other artworks found in Pompeii and Herculaneum is another major challenge. These ancient masterpieces are incredibly fragile and can easily be damaged by exposure to the elements, pollution, and even well-meaning conservation efforts. Specialized techniques and materials are used to clean, stabilize, and protect these artworks, while also ensuring that they remain accessible to the public.

In conclusion, maintaining the ruins of Pompeii and Herculaneum is a complex and ongoing process that requires careful planning, expertise, and resources. By addressing the challenges of size, natural disasters, tourism, and conservation, archaeologists and conservators can protect these ancient sites and ensure that they can be enjoyed by future generations. Through their efforts, the rich recollection, culture, and art of Pompeii and Herculaneum continue to be uncovered and preserved for all to appreciate.

Future Conservation Plans for Pompeii and Herculaneum

As we look towards the future of Pompeii and Herculaneum, it is crucial to consider the conservation efforts needed to preserve these ancient cities for generations to come. Despite the ongoing challenges of natural disasters, tourism, and environmental factors, there are several key strategies that can be implemented to ensure the long-term protection of these invaluable archaeological sites.

One of the primary conservation plans for Pompeii and Herculaneum involves continued excavation and research to uncover more of the cities' hidden treasures. By uncovering and studying new artifacts and structures, archaeologists can learn and comprehend more about the mundane and repetitive life events of the ancient residents and the unbelievable effect of the volcanic explosion that destroyed these cities in 79 AD.

In addition to excavation, conservation efforts will also focus on the preservation and restoration of existing structures and artifacts. This includes stabilizing crumbling walls, protecting fragile frescoes, and implementing advanced conservation techniques to prevent further deterioration. By investing in these preservation efforts, we can ascertain that our children and the generations which will follow have the ability to learn about antiquity and explore the wonders of Pompeii and Herculaneum.

Another crucial aspect of future conservation plans for Pompeii and Herculaneum is sustainable tourism management. With millions of visitors flocking to these sites each year, it is essential to strike a balance between accessibility and preservation. By implementing visitor limits, guided tours, and educational programs, we can protect the integrity of the archaeological sites while still allowing the public to experience their beauty and retrospect.

Lastly, future conservation plans will also involve collaboration with indigenous groups, government agencies, and international organizations to secure funding and support for ongoing preservation efforts. By working together towards a common goal of protecting Pompeii and Herculaneum, we can ensure that these ancient cities continue to inspire and educate people from all walks of life for years to come. In conclusion, the future of Pompeii and Herculaneum relies on a comprehensive and coordinated approach to conservation that prioritizes research, preservation, sustainable tourism, and collaboration. By implementing these strategies, we can protect these remarkable archaeological spots and warrant that they persist a source of ponder and motivation for future generations.

CHAPTER 8: POMPEII AND HERCULANEUM VOLCANIC DETONATION

What Happened to Mount Vesuvius in 79 AD

The upheaval of Mount Vesuvius in 79 AD stands as one of the most infamous natural disasters in narrative of mankind, having engulfed the cities of Pompeii and Herculaneum in a devastating cloud of ash and pumice. This cataclysmic event not only obliterated these ancient Roman cities but also profoundly shaped our archaeological and historical understanding of the region.

The Catastrophic Event

On August 24th, 79 AD, Mount Vesuvius exploded with unprecedented force, sending a massive plume of ash and volcanic debris high into the atmosphere. The volcanic detonation was so powerful that it entrenched Pompeii and Herculaneum under several meters of ash and pumice, effectively preserving them in a state of suspended animation for nearly two millennia. The intense heat caused many buildings to collapse, compounding the destruction wrought by the volcanic debris.

Archaeological Significance

The extraordinary preservation of Pompeii and Herculaneum under layers of ash and debris has provided archaeologists and historians with an unparalleled opportunity to study the culture and civilization of this part of Italy. As if, these two cities have been frozen, petrified, or solidified in time and ashes and debris. Excavations have unearthed a wealth of information about their architecture, art, culture, and religious practices, painting a vivid picture of life before the surge.

- **Architecture:** The well-preserved buildings and urban layouts reveal the sophistication of Roman engineering and design. Public structures such as amphitheaters, bathhouses, and markets highlight the communal and social aspects of Roman life. In contrast, private homes, ranging from modest dwellings to grand villas, display the diversity of living conditions and the importance placed on domestic comfort and luxury.

- **Art and Artifacts:** Artworks including frescoes, mosaics, and sculptures showcase the aesthetic preferences and artistic skills of the period. The vibrant frescoes in the Villa of the Mysteries, for example, depict detailed scenes of religious rituals, offering insight into the spiritual beliefs of the time. Similarly, the intricate mosaics in the House of the Faun reflect Greek cultural prowess and the high value placed on artistic expression.

- **Daily Life:** Cultural artifacts such as pottery, tools, and household utensils provide a window into the everyday routines and culinary practices of the residents. The unearthing of shops and taverns, complete with preserved foodstuffs, sheds light on the economic activities and social interactions that animated these bustling urban centers.

- **Religious Practices:** Numerous temples, shrines, and altars dedicated to deities like Jupiter, Venus, and Mercury indicate the significance of religion in both public and private life. Household shrines found in many homes further underscore the pervasiveness of spiritual devotion among the residents.

Legacy and Guidance

Pompeii and Herculaneum serve as time capsules, offering modern scholars a direct connection to the past and a deeper understanding of the complex and multifaceted nature of Roman society. These sites continue to inspire and educate, highlighting the enduring legacy of these remarkable ancient cities.

The spurt of Mount Vesuvius continues to captivate public imagination, spawning numerous myths and legends. Its impact on modern society is significant, influencing art, literature, and popular culture for centuries. The cuisine, dining practices, and religious beliefs of Pompeii and Herculaneum have been studied in depth, shedding light on the rich cultural heritage of these ancient Roman cities.

The ongoing fascination with Pompeii and Herculaneum not only underscores their historical importance but also ensures that their stories remain a vital part of our collective cultural consciousness. Through continued research and preservation, these ancient cities will continue to offer invaluable insights into the world of ancient Rome for generations to come.

Impact of the Volcanic Ejection on Pompeii and Herculaneum

The sudden release of Mount Vesuvius in 79 AD had a devastating impact on the ruined cities of Pompeii and Herculaneum. The volcanic discharge entombed both cities under a distinct and dense deposit of ash and pumice, sustaining them in an outstanding state of maintenance for epochs to come. The impact of the burst on Pompeii and Herculaneum was profound, forever altering the course of history for these once-thriving Roman settlements.

The jetting of Mount Vesuvius not only covered Pompeii and Herculaneum under tons of volcanic debris but also caused widespread destruction and loss of life. The intense heat and ash clouds generated by the spouting suffocated and killed thousands of residents, leaving behind only their petrified remains. The impact of the projection on Pompeii and Herculaneum was catastrophic, wiping out entire communities in a matter of hours.

The preservation of Pompeii and Herculaneum under layers of volcanic ash and pumice proved to be a double-edged sword. While it provided archaeologists with a unique opportunity to uncover and study these ancient cities, it also presented numerous challenges in terms of excavation and preservation. The impact of the eruption on Pompeii and Herculaneum was both a blessing and a curse, as the same volcanic forces that destroyed the cities also preserved them for future generations to discover.

The spurt of Mount Vesuvius had an eternal impact on the modern understanding of Pompeii and Herculaneum. The meticulous excavation and preservation efforts carried out over the centuries have provided valuable perceptions into the everyday excitements, practices, and beliefs of the ancient residents of these cities. The impact of the blowout on Pompeii and Herculaneum continues to shape our understanding of Roman society and culture, offering a glimpse into the past that would have otherwise been lost to history.

In conclusion, the burst of Mount Vesuvius in 79 AD had a profound impact on the age-old cities of Pompeii and Herculaneum. The catastrophic event laid to rest both cities under a thick layer of ash and pumice, saving them for future generations to uncover. The impact of the volcanic activity on Pompeii and Herculaneum was both destructive and transformative, forever altering the course of history for these once-thriving Roman settlements. Through meticulous excavation and preservation efforts, we continue to uncover the secrets of Pompeii and Herculaneum, shedding light on the daily lives, customs, and beliefs of their ancient residents.

Scientific Discoveries and Research related to the Eruption

The surge of Mount Vesuvius in 79 AD that inhumed the cities of Pompeii and Herculaneum has been the focus of extensive scientific research over the centuries. Archaeologists, geologists, and other experts have worked tirelessly to uncover the mysteries of this catastrophic event and its impact on the ancient world.

One of the most sizable technical breakthroughs related to the volcanic spew is the conservation of the cities themselves. The layers of ash and volcanic debris that covered Pompeii and Herculaneum acted as a natural time capsule, freezing the cities in time and providing researchers with a unique scan into ancient Roman life. The meticulous excavation and preservation efforts have revealed a wealth of information about the daily lives, customs, and beliefs of the inhabitants of these cities.

Geological studies have also shed light on the outbreak itself, helping to create a more accurate timeline of events. By analyzing the composition of the volcanic ash and studying the patterns of destruction in Pompeii and Herculaneum, scientists have been able to reconstruct the sequence of events leading up to the breakout phenomenon and its devastating aftermath.

One of the most fascinating scientific discoveries related to the flux is the study of human remains found in Pompeii and Herculaneum. The shapes of bodies conserved in the ash have furnished useful intuitions into the ending flashes of the inhabitants as they tried to flee the volcano. These remains have helped researchers understand the impact of the volcanic event on the people of Pompeii and Herculaneum and have added a human dimension to the scientific study of the disaster.

In contemporary years, innovations in technology have granted researchers to research even deeper and more extensively into the mysteries of Pompeii and Herculaneum. High-tech imaging

ALIREZAMINAGAR

techniques, DNA analysis, and other cutting-edge methods have enabled scientists to uncover new details about the cities and their inhabitants. These scientific discoveries continue to enhance our understanding of the ancient world and the enduring legacy of Pompeii and Herculaneum.

CHAPTER 9: POMPEII AND HERCULANEUM MYTHS AND LEGENDS

Mythological Stories associated with the Cities Mythological chronicles have always been an essential segment of the history and culture of Pompeii and Herculaneum. These ancient cities were not only centers of commerce and trade but also rich in myths and legends that shaped the beliefs and practices of their inhabitants. One such mythological story associated with Pompeii is the tale of the founding of the city by Hercules, the legendary hero of Greek mythology. According to legend, Hercules founded Pompeii after defeating the giant Cacus and establishing it as a thriving city.

In Herculaneum, the mythological stories revolve around the goddess Venus, who was believed to have had a special connection with the city. It was said that Venus had a temple dedicated to her in Herculaneum, where the inhabitants would offer prayers and sacrifices to ensure her favor and protection. The presence of Venus in the city added to its allure and mystique, making it a place of pilgrimage for those seeking her blessings.

The myths and legends associated with Pompeii and Herculaneum not only added to the cultural richness of these cities but also influenced their art and architecture. Many of the sculptures and frescoes found in the ruins of Pompeii and Herculaneum depict scenes from Greek and Roman mythology, showcasing the importance of these stories in the daily lives of the inhabitants. These artworks served to honor the gods and goddesses believed to have played a role in the prosperity and protection of the cities.

The volcanic discharge event that hid Pompeii and Herculaneum in 79 AD also gave rise to new myths and legends. The sudden and catastrophic destruction of these cities was attributed to the anger of the gods, who were believed to have unleashed their wrath upon the inhabitants for their sins and transgressions. These stories served as a cautionary tale for future generations, warning them of the results of confronting the will power of the divine.

Despite the tragic end of Pompeii and Herculaneum, their myths and legends continue to captivate and inspire people to this day. The stories of Hercules, Venus, and the gods of ancient Rome and Greece have left a lasting legacy on the modern world, shaping our understanding of history, culture, and the human experience. By exploring the mythological stories associated with these lost cities, we can gain a deeper appreciation for their significance and the enduring impact they have had on society.

Folklore and Superstitions surrounding Pompeii and Herculaneum
Folklore and falsehoods have always played a large role in the history and culture of Pompeii and Herculaneum. These ancient cities were not only centers of commerce and daily life but also hubs of supernatural beliefs and legends. From tales of cursed artifacts to stories of vengeful spirits, the folklore surrounding Pompeii and Herculaneum is as intriguing as it is varied.

One of the most famous superstitions surrounding the cities is the belief that the expulsion of Mount Vesuvius in 79 AD was the result of the wrath of the gods. Many residents believed that the volcanic exhalation was a retribution for their crimes and wrongdoings and that they were being disciplined for their immoral behavior. This belief has been perpetuated through various myths and myths passed down over generations.

Another common superstition in Pompeii and Herculaneum is the belief in cursed objects. Many artifacts recovered from the archaeological sites are said to bring bad luck or misfortune to those who possess them. Some locals even believe that the spirits of the ancient residents still linger in the ruins, haunting those who dare to disturb their resting place.

Despite the scientific explanations for the destruction of Pompeii and Herculaneum, the folklore and superstitions surrounding the cities continue to capture the imagination of visitors and locals alike. Whether it is the belief in the power of curses or the fear of vengeful spirits, these stories add an extra layer of mystery to the already fascinating history of the lost cities.

While some may dismiss these superstitions as mere folklore, they serve as a reminder of the deep connection between the past and present in Pompeii and Herculaneum. The myths and legends that have been passed down through generations reflect the enduring impact of these ancient cities on modern society, making them more than just historical sites but living, breathing entities with stories to tell.

Famous Legends about the Destruction of the Cities Throughout history, there have been numerous legends surrounding the demolition of the cities of Pompeii and Herculaneum. One of the most well-known myths is that the outflow of Mount Vesuvius in 79 AD was the result of the gods punishing the inhabitants for their immoral behavior. According to this legend, the cities were home to corruption and vice, and the emission event was a divine retribution for their sins.

Another popular legend is that the gushing of Mount Vesuvius was predicted by the Roman author Pliny the Elder. According to this story, Pliny noticed unusual activity in the days leading up to the projection and warned the residents of Pompeii and Herculaneum to flee. However, his warnings were ignored, and the cities were ultimately destroyed.

There is also a legend that the blowout of Mount Vesuvius was caused by the wrath of the god Vulcan, who was said to live beneath the volcano. According to this myth, Vulcan was angered by the actions of the inhabitants of Pompeii and Herculaneum and unleashed his fury in the form of a devastating expulsion.

One of the most stimulating lores enfolding the destruction of the cities is the story of the "Pompeii Ghosts." According to this legend, the ghosts of the residents who perished in the explosion incident still haunt the ruins of Pompeii and Herculaneum to this day. Many visitors to the sites have reported hearing mysterious voices and seeing shadowy figures moving among the ancient buildings.

While these legends may be fascinating to contemplate, it is important to remember that the true cause of the destruction of Pompeii and Herculaneum was the catastrophic release of Mount Vesuvius. By studying the archaeological evidence and historical records, we can gain a better understanding of the events that led to the downfall of these once-thriving cities.

CHAPTER 10: POMPEII AND HERCULANEUM IMPACT ON MODERN SOCIETY

Predominance of Pompeii and Herculaneum on Art and Literature

The historic cities of Pompeii and Herculaneum have profoundly influenced art and literature throughout passage of time. Their reemergence in the 18th century ignited a renewed fascination with classical art and culture, sparking a resurgence of interest in ancient Roman aesthetics. Since then, artists and writers from the Romantic period onwards have drawn inspiration from these well-preserved ruins, using them as backdrops for their creative works.

Artistic Direction

The art and architecture of Pompeii and Herculaneum have left an indelible mark on modern art and design. The intricate mosaics, vibrant frescoes, and exquisite sculptures found in these cities have inspired countless artists and designers over the centuries. The detailed and colorful artworks of Pompeii and Herculaneum have clouted a choice of artistic movements, from neoclassicism to Art Nouveau, leaving a legacy in the world of art.

Neoclassical artists were captivated by the aesthetic principles and themes seen in these ancient artworks. The symmetry, balance, and classical motifs prevalent in Pompeian and Herculaneum art were incorporated into neoclassical painting, sculpture, and architecture. The ascertainment of these cities provided a tangible link to the classical past, enriching the visual and cultural vocabulary of the time.

Literary Domination

Literature has also been significantly shaped by the discovery and reinvigoration of Pompeii and Herculaneum. The tragic fate of these cities, concealed beneath volcanic ash and preserved in time, has captured the imagination of writers and readers alike. Renowned authors such as Johann Wolfgang von Goethe, Percy Bysshe Shelley, and Alexandre Dumas have woven the stories and settings of Pompeii and Herculaneum into their literary works.

Goethe's travels to Italy and his subsequent writings reflect the profound impact that the ruins had on him. Shelley's poetry often evokes the melancholic beauty of these ancient cities, while Dumas used Pompeii as a dramatic setting in his novel "The Last Days of Pompeii," vividly bringing to life the events leading up to the outwash of Mount Vesuvius.

Cultural and Societal Impact

The leverage of Pompeii and Herculaneum extends beyond the realms of art and literature, impacting modern society's understanding of ancient Roman culture and society. The wealth of information uncovered from these cities has provided unparalleled insights into the daily lives of ordinary Roman citizens, their social structures, and their cultural practices. This deeper understanding has enriched historical and archaeological scholarship, offering a more nuanced view of the past.

Moreover, the preservation and restoration efforts at Pompeii and Herculaneum have set a global standard for archaeological conservation. These efforts underscore the importance of protecting cultural heritage sites, warranting that future generations can learn from and value these invaluable historical treasures.

Enduring Legacy

In conclusion, the persuasion of Pompeii and Herculaneum on art and literature is undeniable. From Romantic poets to contemporary designers, artists and writers have continually drawn inspiration from the ruins of these ancient cities, incorporating their timeless beauty and tragic stories into their works. The legacy of Pompeii and Herculaneum lives on in the art, literature, and culture of today, serving as a powerful reminder of the past's enduring ability to inspire and shape the present. Through their continued study and preservation, these ancient cities will continue to captivate and educate, highlighting the timeless connection between history and creativity.

Popular Culture References to the Lost Cities

Popular Culture References to the Lost Cities of Pompeii and Herculaneum have permeated various forms of media, from movies to music to literature. These ancient cities, tragically entrenched under the ash of Mount Vesuvius in 79 AD, have captivated the imagination of people around the world for centuries.

One of the most well-known references to Pompeii in popular culture is the song "Pompeii" by the British band Bastille. The song's lyrics evoke the sense of loss and destruction that the citizens of Pompeii must have felt as they were engulfed by the volcanic release. The haunting melody and powerful vocals have helped to bring the story of Pompeii to a new generation of listeners.

In film and television, Pompeii and Herculaneum have been featured in numerous productions, including the 2014 movie "Pompeii" starring Kit Harington. The film follows the story of a gladiator who must fight to save his love amidst the chaos of the volcanic outgassing. While the movie takes some creative liberties with historical accuracy, it helps to bring the ancestral settlements to life on the big screen.

Literature has also been swayed and altered by the heartbreak of Pompeii and Herculaneum. Authors such as Robert Harris and Mary Beard have written books that explore the tradition and culture of these lost cities. Their works present helpful visions into the daily life of the residents of Pompeii and Herculaneum, and further clarify their traditions, beliefs and routines.

Overall, the popular culture references to Pompeii and Herculaneum serve as a reminder of the enduring impact of these ancient cities. Through music, film, and literature, people continue to be fascinated by the story of Pompeii and Herculaneum, keeping their memory alive for generations to come. These references help to educate and inspire audiences to learn more about the biography and culture of these remarkable archaeological sites.

L essons Learned from the Tragic Fate of Pompeii and Herculaneum
The tragic fate of Pompeii and Herculaneum provides as a stark recap of the unpredictability of natural calamities and the significance of being primed for such incidents. The upheaval of Mount Vesuvius in 79 AD interred both cities under a substantial deposit of cinders and pumice, saving them in a state of pending animation for centuries. The lessons learned from this disaster are invaluable, not only in terms of historical preservation but also in terms of disaster preparedness for modern societies.

One of the most critical lessons learned from the fate of Pompeii and Herculaneum is the need for effective disaster planning and response mechanisms. The population of these ancient cities had little warning of the impending breakout and overflow of Mount Vesuvius, and as a result, many were caught off guard and perished in the disaster. Today, we have the benefit of advanced technology and scientific knowledge that can help us predict and prepare for natural disasters such as volcanic eruptions. It is essential that communities at risk of such events have comprehensive emergency plans in place to ensure the safety of their residents.

Another lesson to be learned from Pompeii and Herculaneum is the instability and soreness of human civilization in the face of natural forces. The spew of Mount Vesuvius was a catastrophic event that destroyed these thriving cities, wiping out their inhabitants and burying their buildings and artifacts under tons of volcanic debris. This serves as a powerful reminder of the impermanence of human achievements and the need to respect and protect our environment.

The preservation and restoration efforts at Pompeii and Herculaneum also offer valuable lessons in cultural heritage conservation. The painstaking work of excavating and preserving these ancient sites has provided us with a unique sight into the daily lives of the people who lived there nearly 2,000 years ago. The meticulous restoration of buildings, frescoes, and artifacts has allowed us to better understand and appreciate the art, architecture, and culture of these lost cities.

In conclusion, the tragic fate of Pompeii and Herculaneum has left us with a wealth of knowledge and insights that continue to inform and inspire us today. By studying the events that led to their destruction, we can learn valuable lessons about disaster preparedness, cultural heritage preservation, and the resilience of human civilization in the face of adversity. These lost cities serve as strong reminders and witnesses to the persistent command of the human character and vitality and a tell us about the value of learning from the past to shape a better future.

CHAPTER 11: POMPEII AND HERCULANEUM CUISINE AND DINING

C ulinary Traditions in Pompeii and Herculaneum
Culinary traditions in Pompeii and Herculaneum offer a fascinating view to their diet and foods in those once-vibrant cities. From street food vendors to elaborate banquets, food played a central role in the social and cultural fabric of these bustling urban centers. The culinary practices of Pompeii and Herculaneum were directed by a variety of factors, including trade routes, agricultural practices, and cultural exchanges with other regions of the Roman Empire.

In Pompeii and Herculaneum, food was not just sustenance, but also a form of social currency. Banquets, known as "convivia," were a common occurrence in the homes of the wealthy and elite. These lavish feasts featured a wide array of dishes, including meats, seafood, fruits, vegetables, and exotic spices imported from distant lands. Guests reclined on couches while enjoying the food and entertainment provided by musicians, dancers, and actors.

Street food was also popular in Pompeii and Herculaneum, with vendors selling a variety of snacks and quick meals to residents and visitors alike. Foods such as bread, olives, cheese, and honey cakes were readily available from street stalls and food carts throughout the cities. In addition to traditional Roman fare, the culinary landscape of Pompeii and Herculaneum was shaped by persuasions from other cultures, including Greek, Egyptian, and Syrian cuisines.

The volcanic breakout of Mount Vesuvius in 79 AD not only destroyed Pompeii and Herculaneum but also preserved a wealth of information about the daily lives of their inhabitants, including their culinary practices. Archaeological excavations have uncovered well-preserved food remains, including carbonized bread, fish bones, and fruit pits, providing valuable insights into the diet and eating habits of the ancient Romans.

Today, visitors to Pompeii and Herculaneum can experience the culinary traditions of these legendary urban centers through guided tours, museum exhibits, and recreated ancient recipes. By exploring the food and dining practices of Pompeii and Herculaneum, we can gain a deeper understanding of the rich cultural heritage of these lost cities and their enduring impact on modern society.

F ood and Drink of the Ancient Romans
Food and drink were an integral part of daily life in ancient Rome, and the residents of Pompeii and Herculaneum were no exception. The diet of the ancient Romans was varied and rich in flavors, reflecting the miscellaneous culinary effects of the Mediterranean region. From simple bread and olives to elaborate feasts with exotic ingredients, the people of Pompeii and Herculaneum enjoyed a wide range of foods.

One of the staples of the ancient Roman nutrition was bread, which was made from wheat flour and cooked in collective ovens.

The bread was often seasoned with herbs and served with olive oil for dipping. Olives were another common food in ancient Rome, and they were eaten both as a snack and as an ingredient in many dishes. The Romans also enjoyed a diversity of fruits, including figs, grapes, and pomegranates.

Meals in ancient Rome typically consisted of three courses: a starter, a primary course, and a dessert. The main course often featured meats such as pork, beef, or fish, which were seasoned with herbs and spices. Vegetables such as beans, lentils, and cabbage were also popular. For dessert, the Romans enjoyed sweets such as honey cakes, dates, and nuts.

Wine was the preferred drink of the ancient Romans, and it was consumed in large quantities at meals and social gatherings. The Romans believed that wine was a gift from the gods and that it had both medicinal and religious significance. In Pompeii and Herculaneum, wine was manufactured locally and exported to other regions of the Roman Empire.

Overall, the food and drink of the ancient Romans played a significant role in their daily lives and social interactions. The cuisine of Pompeii and Herculaneum reflects the culinary sophistication and cultural diversity of the ancient Roman world. By studying the food and drink of these lost cities, we can gain a better understanding of the people who lived there and the way they experienced the world through their senses.

Dining Habits and Customs in the Cities
In the antiquated cities of Pompeii and Herculaneum, dining habits and customs played a significant role in daily life. The people of these bustling Roman cities enjoyed a rich culinary tradition that was influenced by a variety of factors, including social status, cultural exchange, and access to

ingredients. Dining was not just about nutrition, but also about socializing, entertaining guests, and showcasing wealth and status.

One of the most striking aspects of dining in Pompeii and Herculaneum was the importance placed on communal meals. Families and friends often gathered to share a meal, which was seen as a way to strengthen bonds and foster a sense of community. Banquets and feasts were common, especially among the wealthy elite, who used these lavish events to display their wealth and social standing.

The food that was consumed in Pompeii and Herculaneum was varied and flavorful, reflecting the diverse inspirations of the Roman Empire. Common ingredients included grains, legumes, fruits, vegetables, fish, and meat. Olive oil, wine, and honey were popular staples in the diet, and were often used in cooking and as condiments. Spices and herbs were also regularly utilized to make the dishes more tasty.

Dining out was also a popular pastime in Pompeii and Herculaneum, with a variety of eateries catering to different tastes and budgets. Taverns, restaurants, and snack bars dotted the streets of these ancient cities, offering a wide range of dishes and drinks to patrons. Street vendors and food stalls were also common, providing ready and accessible selections for those active and busy.

Overall, dining in Pompeii and Herculaneum was a multi-faceted and dynamic experience that reflected the rich cultural tapestry of these ancient Roman cities. From communal meals to lavish banquets, from simple street food to elaborate feasts, the dining habits and customs of Pompeii and Herculaneum offer a fascinating observe into the daily life of these lost cities.

CHAPTER 12: POMPEII AND HERCULANEUM RELIGIOUS PRACTICES AND BELIEFS

Gods and Goddesses worshipped in Pompeii and Herculaneum

In the historic cities of Pompeii and Herculaneum, religion was integral to daily life, deeply embedded in practices and routines of the inhabitants. The people worshipped a varied pantheon of gods and goddesses, each overseeing specific domains and possessing distinct attributes. These deities were believed to wield immense power, influencing various aspects of life, from fertility and agriculture to war and craftsmanship.

The Pantheon of Gods and Goddesses

The religious landscape of Pompeii and Herculaneum was rich and varied, reflecting the polytheistic nature of Roman religion. Major deities like Jupiter, the king of the gods, were revered for their supreme power and authority over the heavens. Venus, the goddess of love and beauty, was venerated for her weight on personal relationships and fertility. Mars, the god of war, was invoked for protection and victory in battles, while Minerva, the goddess of wisdom and craftsmanship, was honored for her guidance in intellectual pursuits and skilled labor.

Temples and Shrines

Temples dedicated to these gods and goddesses were prominent in both cities, serving as centers of worship and community gatherings. The Temple of Jupiter in Pompeii, for instance, stood majestically in the forum, symbolizing the city's devotion to the chief deity. Alongside grand temples, smaller household shrines, known as lararia, were found in many homes. These private altars allowed families to worship domestic spirits and household gods, ensuring their favor and protection in daily life.

Religious Practices and Rituals

Religious practices in Pompeii and Herculaneum included a range of rituals and ceremonies designed to appease the gods and seek their blessings. Sacrifices, both animal and, occasionally, human, were common, as were offerings of food, wine, and incense. Festivals and public celebrations were also integral to religious life, marking important events and honoring various deities. The festival of Vinalia, for example, celebrated the grape harvest and was dedicated to Jupiter and Venus, reflecting the agricultural roots of these communities.

Artistic Depictions

The guidance of religion stretched into the art and architecture of Pompeii and Herculaneum. Frescoes and mosaics often depicted scenes from mythology and religious rituals, providing visual representations of the gods and their stories. The frescoes in the Villa of the Mysteries in Pompeii, which illustrate the initiation rites of a mystery cult, offer profound insights into the spiritual and religious experiences of the time.

Social and Cultural Impact

Religion in Pompeii and Herculaneum was not only a spiritual pursuit but also a means of reinforcing social cohesion and community identity. Public worship and festivals brought people together, fostering a sense of shared cultural and religious heritage. The integration of religious symbols and practices into daily life underscored the omnipresence of the divine in every aspect of existence.

In summary, religion in

Pompeii and Herculaneum were cornerstones of daily life, shaping the social and cultural fabric of these ancient cities. The inhabitants worshipped a diverse pantheon of gods and goddesses, each overseeing specific domains and believed to prowess numerous views of life.

The Pantheon of Gods and Goddesses

The religious landscape of Pompeii and Herculaneum was rich and varied, reflecting the polytheistic nature of Roman religion. Major deities like Jupiter, the king of the gods, were revered for their supreme power and authority over the heavens. Venus, the goddess of love and beauty, was venerated for her clout and command on personal relationships and fertility. Mars, the god of war, was invoked for protection and victory in battles, while Minerva, the goddess of wisdom and craftsmanship, was honored for her guidance in intellectual pursuits and skilled labor.

Temples and Shrines

Temples dedicated to these gods and goddesses were prominent in both cities, serving as centers of worship and community gatherings. The Temple of Jupiter in Pompeii, for instance, stood majestically in the forum, symbolizing the city's devotion to the chief deity. Alongside grand temples, smaller household shrines, known as lararia, were found in many homes. These private altars allowed families to worship domestic spirits and household gods, ensuring their favor and protection in daily life.

Religious Practices and Rituals

Religious practices in Pompeii and Herculaneum included a range of rituals and ceremonies designed to appease the gods and seek their blessings. Sacrifices, both animal and, occasionally, human, were common, as were offerings of food, wine, and incense. Festivals and public celebrations were also integral to religious life, marking important events and honoring various deities. The festival of Vinalia, for example, celebrated the grape harvest and was dedicated to Jupiter and Venus, reflecting the agricultural roots of these communities.

Artistic Depictions

The authority of religion extended into the art and architecture of Pompeii and Herculaneum. Frescoes and mosaics often depicted scenes from mythology and religious rituals, providing visual representations of the gods and their stories. The frescoes in the Villa of the Mysteries in Pompeii, which illustrate the initiation rites of a mystery cult, offer profound insights into the spiritual and religious experiences of the time.

Social and Cultural Impact

Religion in Pompeii and Herculaneum was not only a spiritual pursuit but also a means of reinforcing social cohesion and community identity. Public worship and festivals brought people together, fostering a sense of shared cultural and religious heritage. The integration of religious symbols and practices into daily life underscored the omnipresence of the divine in every aspect of existence.

In summary, religion in Pompeii and Herculaneum was a vital aspect of daily life, permeating the art, lifestyle, and social structures of these ancient cities. The worship of a diverse pantheon of gods and goddesses, along with the rich array of rituals and ceremonies, highlights the deep spiritual devotion of their inhabitants and offers a window into the complex and multifaceted nature of Roman society.

Rituals and Formalities in the Temples and Shrines

Rituals and ceremonies were common events among the residents of Pompeii and Herculaneum. Temples and shrines were central to the daily lives of the people, who sought the favor of their gods through offerings and prayers. These revered places were not only homes of worship, but also served as community congregation spots where ceremonies were held to honor the deities.

The temples and shrines in Pompeii and Herculaneum were intricately planned and decorated with exquisite drawings and architecture. The residents of these cities spared no expense in constructing these sacred spaces, which were meant to inspire awe and reverence in those who visited them. The temples were dedicated to a variety of gods and goddesses, each with their own ceremonies and services associated with them.

One of the most crucial practices in the temples and shrines was the offering of sacrifices to the gods. Animals, such as sheep and pigs, were commonly sacrificed to show devotion and seek favor from the deities. These sacrifices were often acted by priests or priestesses, who proceeded as mediators between the individuals and the gods. The blood of the sacrificed creatures was assumed to satisfy the gods and warrant their protection and blessings upon the city.

Ceremonies were also held in the temples and shrines to mark important occasions, such as religious festivals or the changing of seasons. These ceremonies typically involved processions, music, dance, and feasting, and were meant to bring the community together in celebration and worship. The residents of Pompeii and Herculaneum took great pride in their religious practices and beliefs, and these ceremonies were a way for them to express their devotion to the gods and goddesses.

Overall, the temples and shrines of Pompeii and Herculaneum were central to the religious and cultural life of the ancient residents. These sacred spaces were not only places of worship, but also served as community hubs where rituals and ceremonies were performed to honor the gods and seek their favor. The intricate design and elaborate rituals of these temples and shrines reflect the deep religious beliefs and practices of the people who once called these lost cities home.

Religious Persuasion on City Dwellers' Everyday Lives

Religion played a significant role in the daily life of the inhabitants of Pompeii and Herculaneum, two ancient Roman cities that were covered by the volcanic flux, gases, and ashes exiting from Mount Vesuvius in 79 AD. The people of these cities worshipped a variety of gods and goddesses, including the Roman pantheon as well as local deities. Temples devoted to these gods and goddesses were a common sight in both Pompeii and Herculaneum, operating as spots of devotion and community rally.

In Pompeii, one of the most prominent religious structures is the Temple of Apollo, located near the Forum. This temple was offered to the god Apollo, the supporter of music, poetry, and rebuilding. The people of Pompeii would come to the temple to pray for healing, seek guidance, and make offerings to the god. Similarly, in Herculaneum, the Temple of the Augustales was a place of worship for the cult of the Roman emperor Augustus. This cult played a meaningful role in the spiritual and political life of the city.

Religious festivals and rituals were also an important part of daily life in Pompeii and Herculaneum. The people of these cities would participate in ceremonies to honor their gods and goddesses, such as the festival of Saturnalia in honor of the god Saturn. During these festivals, the streets would be filled with music, dancing, and feasting as the people celebrated their religious beliefs and traditions.

The sway of religion extended beyond the temples and festivals, shaping the social and moral fabric of Pompeii and Herculaneum. The faith in an life after death and the significance of appropriate interment practices were central tenets of Roman religion. The people of these cities would bury their dead with care and perform rituals to ensure the safe passage of the deceased to the underworld. These religious beliefs helped to provide a sense of order and continuity in the face of the uncertainty of daily life.

In short, religion did play a profound role in life in Pompeii and Herculaneum, a multifaceted and many-sided role. From the temples dedicated to the gods and goddesses to the festivals and rituals that brought the community together, religion played a central role in shaping the cultural and social landscape of these ancient cities. The beliefs and practices of the people of Pompeii and Herculaneum reflected their hopes, fears, and aspirations, providing insight into the spiritual world of the Roman Empire.

CHAPTER 13: CONCLUSION

Recap of Key Points about Pompeii and Herculaneum

Now, let us review certain resolution points about the old metropolises of Pompeii and Herculaneum. These two cities, located in present-day Italy, were both submerged by the outburst of Mount Vesuvius in 79 AD, preserving them in an amazing state of conservation for centuries.

One of the most charming sides of Pompeii and Herculaneum is their architecture. Both cities were well-planned and had impressive public buildings, such as theaters, temples, and baths. The residences of the prosperous were decorated with charming frescoes and mosaics, giving us a survey into the artistic tastes of the ancient Romans.

The daily life of the residents of Pompeii and Herculaneum is also a key point of interest. From the remains of bakeries and taverns to the graffiti scrawled on the walls, we can piece together a picture of how life was going on in these cities nearly 2,000 years ago. The exploration and examination of preserved food and household items gives us insight into the diet and customs of the ancient inhabitants.

The spasm of Mount Vesuvius in 79 AD had a dreadful shock on Pompeii and Herculaneum, burying them under tons of volcanic ash and pumice. The suddenness of the explosion and outrageous activity meant that many residents were caught unaware and off-guard, leading to a tragic loss of life. The cities were largely forgotten until their reidentification in the 18th century, sparking renewed interest in the ancient world.

Today, Pompeii and Herculaneum are popular destinations for tourists and archaeologists alike. The enduring conservation and refurbishment attempts make sure that forthcoming generations will be able to persist in learning from these incredible sites. The myths and legends surrounding the cities, as well as their impact on modern society, continue to intrigue and inspire us.

Final Thoughts on the Lost Cities
In conclusion, the lost cities of Pompeii and Herculaneum continue to captivate and intrigue both historians and tourists alike. These ancient Roman cities were frozen in time by the tragic explosion of Mount Vesuvius in 79 AD, offering us a unique flash into the daily events of the people who once inhabited them. From the well-preserved buildings and artifacts to the tragic and haunting plaster casts of the volcano's victims, there is no shortage of wonders to explore and ponder in these archaeological sites.

The art and architecture of Pompeii and Herculaneum are a proof to the competence and imagination of the ancient Romans. Intricate frescoes, mosaics, and sculptures adorn the walls and floors of homes and public buildings, showcasing the rich cultural heritage of these cities. The layout and design of the urban spaces also reveal insights into the social hierarchy and daily routines of the inhabitants, shedding light on their values and priorities.

One cannot discuss Pompeii and Herculaneum without mentioning the devastating volcanic eruption that immersed them under layers of ash and pumice. The sudden and violent nature of this event operates as an absolute notice of the power and unpredictability of mother nature. The preservation and restoration efforts of modern archaeologists have allowed us to piece together the stories of these lost cities and honor the memory of those who perished in the disaster.

The myths and legends surrounding Pompeii and Herculaneum add another layer of intrigue to their backstory. From tales of hidden treasure to ghostly apparitions haunting the ruins, these stories capture the imagination and fuel our fascination with the past. While some of these legends may be based in truth, others serve as cautionary tales about the dangers of hubris and complacency.

In closing, the impact of Pompeii and Herculaneum on modern society cannot be overplayed. These ancient cities have inspired countless works of art, literature, and film, sparking a renewed interest in Roman history and folkways. By preserving and studying these archaeological sites, we honor the legacy of those who came before us and ensure that their stories will continue to be told for generations to come.

R esources for Further Exploration
To further explore the fascinating archives and beliefs of Pompeii and Herculaneum, there are a wealth of resources available to the public and layman. Whether you are interested in archaeological tours, art and architecture, ancient daily life, preservation and restoration, or the impact of these lost cities on modern society, there are numerous avenues for delving deeper into the mysteries of Pompeii and Herculaneum.

One valuable resource for those looking to learn more about Pompeii and Herculaneum is the official website of the

Archaeological Park of Pompeii. This website provides a wealth of information on the history and habits of these ancient cities, as well as details on current excavation projects and upcoming events. Additionally, the website offers virtual tours and interactive exhibits that allow visitors to explore the ruins from the comfort of their own home.

For those interested in experiencing Pompeii and Herculaneum in person, there are several archaeological tours available that offer guided visits to the ruins. These tours are directed by experienced experts who can afford appreciated understandings into the chronicle and significance of these ancient cities. Additionally, many tour companies offer specialized tours that focus on specific aspects of Pompeii and Herculaneum, such as their art and architecture, daily life, or religious practices.

In addition to official resources, there are several books and documentaries available that delve into the vestiges and norms of Pompeii and Herculaneum. Books such as "The Fires of Vesuvius" by Mary Beard and "Pompeii: The Day a City Died" by Robert Etienne offer in-depth examinations of these lost cities, while documentaries like "Pompeii: The Last Day" provide a visual exploration of the events leading up to the catastrophic eruption of Mount Vesuvius.

For those interested in exploring the culinary traditions of Pompeii and Herculaneum, there exist a few resources available that explore the cuisine and dining practices of these ancient cities. Books such as "Pompeii's Table: The Lost Recipes of Ancient Rome" by Francine Segan provide insight into the foods and flavors of Pompeii and Herculaneum, while culinary tours of the region offer the opportunity to sample traditional dishes and learn about the culinary narrative of the area. Whether you are a antiquity buff, an art enthusiast, or simply curious about the daily lives of ancient Romans, there are countless resources available for further exploring the lost cities of Pompeii and Herculaneum. By taking advantage of these resources, you can learn and understand the rich epoch, beliefs, and worth of these remarkable archaeological sites.

Printed in Great Britain
by Amazon